The Dearne District Light Railways

By
C.T. Goode

ISBN 1 870313 18 6
72 Woodland Drive, Anlaby, Hull. HU10 7HX

Burstwick Print & Publicity Services
13a Anlaby Road, Hull. HU1 2PJ

Foreword

I wrote my first book on the Mexborough & Swinton Traction Co. in 1982, at a time when, up to then I knew next to nothing about its neighbour, the Dearne District; in fact I had passed my boyhood in Doncaster in ignorance of the system probably due, in fairness, to the short period during which it existed. Research for this little work was helped on by the booklet by Mr. Denton of 1980, which gave the line some life and character, and by odd letters from local, now elderly travellers on the tramway who gave encouragement. There were plenty of photos, (these are needed first to provide a skeleton on which to hang the words), but some of the local authorities, while willing enough to assist nowadays, demand such high copying and repro. fees that costs for a work of this modest size are soon inflated. Enquiries so far have failed to unearth the sight of any tickets or timetables for the DDLR. I hope that they do not appear, following one of the Golden Rules of this enterprise, whereby useful information is withheld until well after publication, as has indeed happened in the past. I hope that the choice of photos' is correctly captioned for the locations, as several were not at all. Provenance was also tricky in some cases.

My thanks are due to the Archivists of the various Dearne Authorities and of Rotherham, also to Mrs. Raybould of Yorkshire Traction Publicity Office, Falkirk Museums and Blackpool Libraries.

And now let us allow the little trams to rattle once more round the curve northwards and over the canal bridge in Wath to journey's end.

C. Tony Goode.

Anlaby, Hull. October 1997.

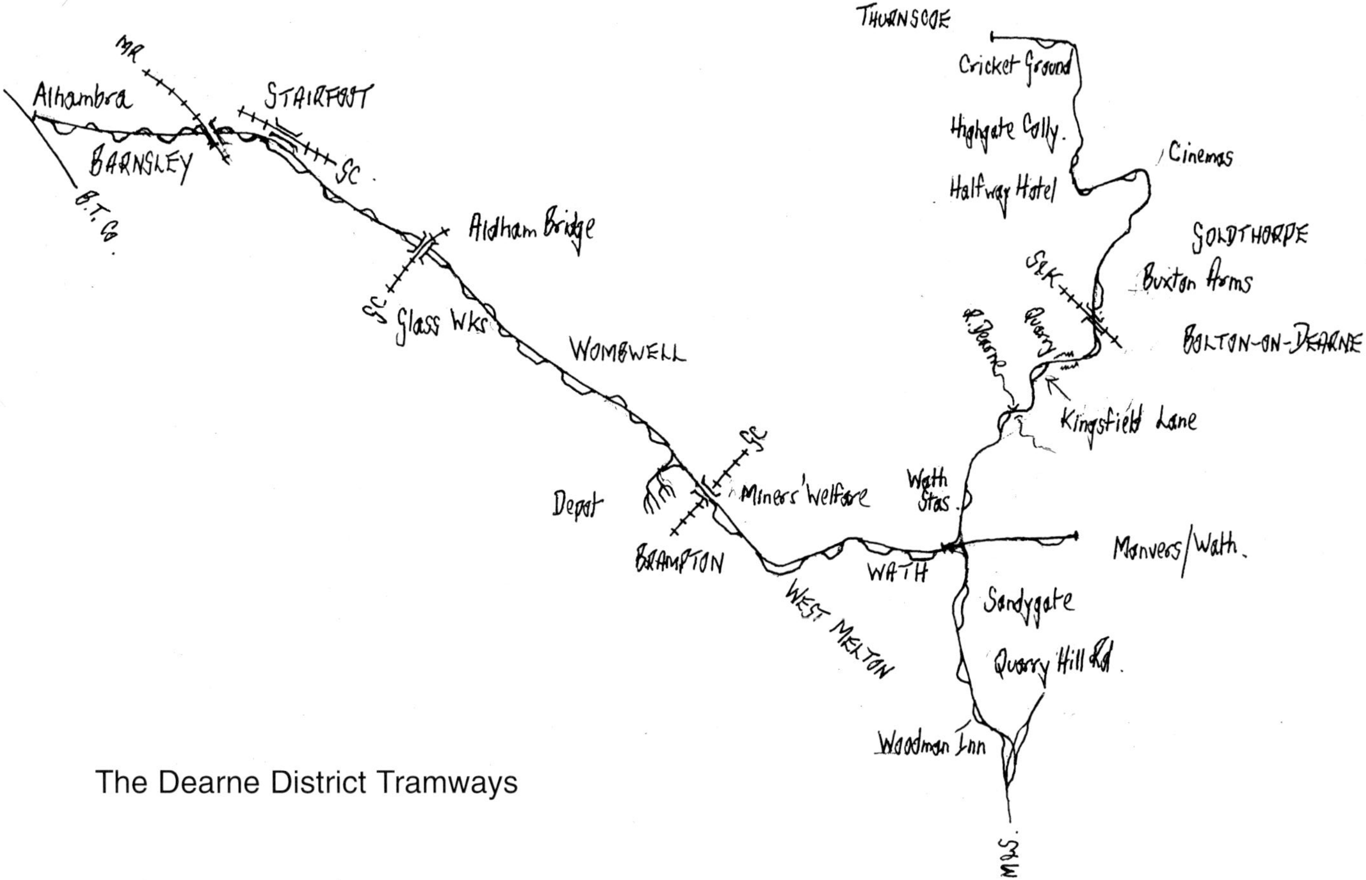

The Dearne District Tramways

The Dearne District Light Railway

Chapters:

Front Cover

Local menfolk watch No. 17 pass in High Street Wombwell

Lens of Sutton

Abbreviations:

DDLR	The Dearne District Light Railways.
DVR	The Dearne Valley Railway.
GCR	The Great Central Railway.
GEC	The General Electric Company.
L & Y	The Lancashire & Yorkshire Railway.
MR	The Midland Railway.
MS & L	The Manchester, Sheffield & Lincolnshire Railway.
M & ST	The Mexborough & Swinton Traction Company.
S & K	The Swinton & Knottingley Joint Line (Midland & North Eastern).

Topography and Railway Background

Before the tram begins to rattle and, indeed, before the trains begin to puff, a little scene setting is in order. The West Riding of Yorkshire, that vast area which encompassed what many people besides Winifred Holtby called the South Riding, was well placed in the eastern lee of the Pennines with four major rivers, the Wharfe, Aire, Calder and Don, themselves fed by many small streams which were fast flowing and with soft water which was ideal for the washing of wool used in the weaving industry which grew in its earliest form in homesteads in the eighteenth century. Coal was won in small quantities from much earlier, in the twelfth century and was transported by the water-ways from the Elizabethan period, while ironstone was mined from the fourteenth century and smelted in woodland areas using charcoal ovens. To the south grew the cutlery industry of Sheffield using water power to drive the mill machinery.

A significant development came along in the eighteenth century when steam power began to replace water as a driving force, while the use of coal as a fuel for raising steam drove engines in both the cutlery and weaving factories. The domestic production of wool weaving moved from individual houses to larger factories which were built near rivers and streams and closer to the new coal mines. Logical progression saw the development of turnpike roads for which tolls were charged to enable their upkeep, canals which often linked rivers together and railways which were initially horse powered, running on plates of stone or wood. The first of these was most likely Lord Middleton's which ran on his estate from Wollaton colliery, Nottingham, south to the canal nearby. In the West Riding the first wagon way was the Middleton Railway of 1758, followed by the Heck & Wentbridge (near Pontefract) of 1826.

The West Riding was well provided with raw materials, hills for the sheep to graze upon and produce the wool, stone for the houses and factories and coal and iron ore waiting to be mined by an honest and willing work force. The whole of the worsted manufacture transferred itself en block from East Anglia to new sites by the Aire and Calder.

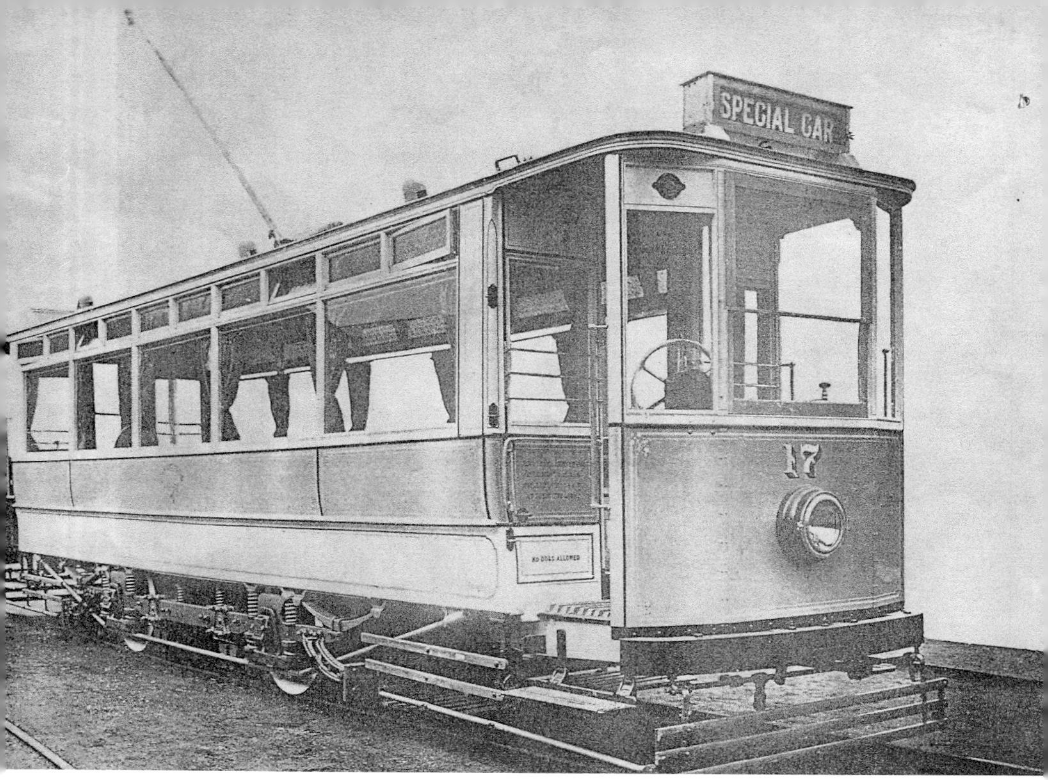

A Works Photograph of No.17 *Dick, Kerr, Preston.*

Barnsley would always rate itself as a part of South Yorkshire, being in many ways more linked to Doncaster and Rotherham than to Huddersfield or Wakefield, probably due to the division caused by the hills. Daniel Defoe, of Robinson Crusoe fame, is said to have referred to the town as 'Black Barnsley' in 1727, due to the coal mines and ironworks which were to be found there in some number even then, in fact 'black' may well have been an error for 'bleak' as the town was an exposed place set on a hillside, as today. 'Bleach' might also be considered, as the town had several bleaching and dyeing works within it, though relatively few collieries or ironworks. One of the most important coal seams lay just outside the town, known as the Silkstone after the village some four miles away. The seam runs along the valley of the river Dearne, a minor water course flowing eastwards to Wath, near where it flows into the Don.

Barnsley Exchange Station. A passenger would be entertained either by the bus station at his back or by the display of the loco depot in front of him. A curious operating layout. Note the GC signal and Jumble Lane signal box with its peculiar canopy.
Photo: GCRS Collection

From 41,000 in 1901 Barnsley numbered 76,783 in 1993 and has always been a remarkably active and friendly town. Clean and tidy, despite the gloominess of its surrounding area, there is contrast in the cluster of newer buildings round the Town Hall, built by Briggs & Thornely in 1933 in the London Transport style of the period. It possesses a fine tower which dominates the skyline and a council chamber which is as good as the best in the land. Nearby is the College of Mining & Technology, and the Cooper Art Gallery. One of Barnsley's famous sons was Joseph Locke, not the singer but the railway engineer who must rank with George Stephenson. In his memory his wife gave the park, which bears the family name, to the town in 1861.

An up-to-date feature of the town is the obligatory shopping centre, a brand new affair of shining metal and glass built on the site of the Alhambra cinema.

Villages were numerous, but journeys between even the closest ones were surprisingly infrequent, due quite often to the state of the roads or to sheer self-sufficiency. There was little desire to wander afield and explore, unless one were in trade and wished to market produce or crafts. The stage coach, once a day or perhaps just once or twice a week, was slow but reliable and catered for those who would visit other places. The railway was to provide more accessibility for all, and an early comer was the Leeds & Selby which was a short run, linked like many of the early projects, to a waterway at Selby. More famous, the Liverpool & Manchester Railway was an important development between two great cities, begun around 1835. Nearer home was the North Midland Railway which, in 1846 opened a line between Derby and Leeds and, at its southern extremity linked into the London and Birmingham line, thus opening up the potential of markets in Yorkshire and the capital. However, little was provided for Sheffield, since George Stephenson who engineered the line believed in keeping things as flat and as straight as possible, so avoided tunnelling into the city but passed to the east instead. From the north came the first of George Hudson's lines, the York & North Midland from Newcastle and Edinburgh, reaching the North Midland at Normanton, a modest place which found a few early years of glory as a 'service stop' for passengers requiring sustenance en route. To this place also came the Manchester & Leeds along the Calder valley through Mirfield; they found that, to reach Leeds they had to share the same lines as the North Midland from Normanton. The M & L became the Lancashire & Yorkshire in due course and was noted initially for poor railway practice and spartan rolling stock.

The Barnsley coalfield and its villages were now being approached by new railway lines which ran to the north of the area, the nearest being the NMR which passed through Cudworth, some four miles away, and Wath-on-Dearne. The last of the lines opened in 1845 locally was the Sheffield, Ashtonunder-Lyne & Manchester (try fitting that on a small wagon) which ran to the south of the area via Woodhead tunnel and Penistone, proceeding beyond Sheffield to Grimsby and Cleethorpes. Towns in the West Riding were eventually reached from these lines; Barnsley from Penistone, Sheffield from Rotherham, Halifax from the M & L on a route which was eventually extended to Bradford. Alone of all the upstarts who had entered the area as if to rob it of its mineral wealth was the South Yorkshire Railway, a child of local coal owners, provided to connect Barnsley and its mines with Sheffield and Doncaster. This route was extended to Grimsby and became in time, along with the SA & M the Manchester, Sheffield & Lincolnshire Railway, offering Barnsley an important link with London and the North via the Great Northern at Doncaster. The latter company seemed to keep its distance, as did one of the country's most important lines, the London & North Western which entered Leeds first of all only as a joint line with the L & Y through Mirfield.

Barnsley Court House. A decent, covered station set on an embankment. The DMU would be going to Sheffield via Chapeltown *Photo: GCRS Collection*

Wath G.C. station from the road bridge looking east towards Manvers Main. *C.T. Goode*

Of more use and significance in the area of the Barnsley coal field was the coming of the Swinton & Knottingley Joint Railway, opened in 1879, a well laid and thoughtfully planned trunk route from York to Sheffield. Here was a product of the North Eastern and Midland companies who built solid stations at Pontefract Baghill, Moorthorpe & South Elmsall, Frickley, and Bolton-on-Dearne. The reason behind these stations in relation to each other is somewhat vague. Pontefract obviously served a large population. As far as the others were concerned, it is doubtful whether much interchange took place. Moorthorpe was popular for holiday traffic on summer Saturdays, while Bolton would generate local journeys, perhaps to Rotherham for social or shopping outings. Later on, the station was known as 'for Goldthorpe', the latter village being a good walk away. Frickley was a loser from the outset, not even having a place of that name nearby, only the Hall and a hamlet, Clayton. The site lay too far north to benefit the mining village of Thurnscoe and yet the line passed through between that village and Goldthorpe, an ideal location which was missed for some reason, but which has happily been remedied in recent months with the provision of halts. Possibly such stations were originally sited to attract farm traffic and with little idea of any possible mass housing coming to the district.

The little Hull & Barnsley Railway did its bit when it built a branch down from its own main line near Kirk Smeaton southwards to Wath, where a small terminus was built near the other two companies' stations. On the way it also passed by Thurnscoe adjacent to the S & K and had the enterprise to provide the little station of Hickleton & Thurnscoe which was quite centrally placed in the latter village, more decorative than practical, as what was on offer was very sparse and not too inviting.

Bolton-on-Dearne Station looking south. C.T. Goode

And so the railways had arrived at different times, their presence allowing existing industries to grow larger and permitting easier despatch of products from new sidings run into the works yards. With cloth mills, spinning and weaving could now be carried out in separate places, then brought together by means of the railway. Small mines using primitive tram roads were gradually closed as bigger collieries were opened alonside the railways along the deeper coal seams which ran from west to east, the deepest coal being found in the east. These measures were found and worked until the late twenties.

Socially, the population had doubled in the second half of the nineteenth century, with the workforce living close to its employer and having neither the time nor the inclination to travel far. Day returns and runabout tickets were unheard of; nowadays, each Sunday in summer our local bus company runs day excursions and mystery trips for £3.50 or so, a thing undreamed of a century ago. The managerial staff would have lived away from the fumes and smoke up on the hills, without rail access but with the family gig to help out. Some there were who became early rail commuters, travelling to and from residences in Ilkley and Harrogate, even from the Fylde coast to their mills in Manchester. For the workers there were commuter branch lines, with frequent services between Huddersfield and Holmfirth, Clayton West and Meltham operated by the L & Y, the company already mentioned for its dire rolling stock. However, its wheels turned with efficiency. The sole LNWR branch worked from Huddersfield served Kirkburton.

Trams in Barnsley. Local Schemes

There was no such luxury for Barnsley folk who had either to live 'over the shop' or walk or cycle to work. Even the location of the town was treated with some frivolity at first, as Cudworth was the nearest station at four miles away on the NMR, due to Stephenson's obsession with flatness and straight lines. Eventually the town was linked by a branch push-and-pull service, opened to passengers in June 1870 which earned its keep, making 22 runs on weekdays and eight on Sundays in 1914, with the occasional run through to Wakefield.

Barnsley acquired its own station with the opening of Exchange (Regent St.) to traffic in February 1857 at the end of the $6^1/_2$ mile MS & L branch from Penistone, an important stop on the Sheffield - Manchester line. Exchange was owned by the L & YR and soon the line was extended round the town into the Midland station at Court House, where the property was to be jointly owned. MS & L trains began to run to Court House on the same day as did the MR. In 1864 MS & L interests took on a half share of the L & Y station, to which the latter company's services had been running from Wakefield since January 1850. This station was very basic in nature and the L & Y were prevailed upon to make improvements in 1870 and, of course, the MS & L at this time enjoyed the option of working in and out of the two adjacent high and low level stations.

In 1914 the L & Y had 12 trains running each way to Wakefield Kirkgate, with three extended to and from Leeds. There were two extras on Saturdays only and three each on Sundays. In the same year the MS & L at Court House station ran nine trains on weekdays and three on Sundays to either Mexborough or Doncaster, with two arrivals at Barnsley from Penistone on weekdays. In the opposite direction eleven arrived at Barnsley from Mexborough, these connecting with Doncaster-Sheffield services there. Three trains were all-station stoppers from Barnetby. More detail is given below when the Wombwell services are discussed.

Car No. 14 outside the Car Barns (depot) in Brampton Road, Wombwell. *Photo: C.F. Massingham*

The last important service for the area did not commence until 1897. This was the MR service from Court House to Sheffield via Chapeltown and Wombwell, a later option for the service to Sheffield via Cudworth. Here 12 services went to Sheffield Midland and 11 returned, with extras on Saturdays only and three each way on Sundays. An odd morning run left for Chapeltown at 8.32 am., returning by 9.14 am. - all this in 1914.

The story of local electric traction begins in Barnsley when, in 1903 a prospectus appeared offering shares in the Barnsley & District Electric Traction Company, registered on 3rd March 1902, to take over the new undertakings set out in the Barnsley & District Light Railway Orders of 1980 and Extension Order of 1902. Behind both of these was British Electric Traction, a company fostered for rather obvious reasons by the Brush Electrical

Engineering Company in 1896 to promote new tramway schemes and thereby to market its own products. It was not always possible to persuade local councils to take on the running of such schemes, as there were competing lighting, sewage and hospital projects all vying for often limited finances in these enterprising times. Often, therefore, it was a wise move to let BET keep a controlling hand on developments, in the knowledge that, in the event of difficulties, they would shoulder the financial risks.

Barnsley's operation was a modest one, and ten vehicles were obtained for the four miles, one furlong route which ran from Old Mill lane in the Smithies area of the north east via Court House and Eldon street to Worsbrough Bridge and Dale along a final division of the route into two. There were serious running-in problems with sanding gear, brakes and electrical insulation, so that two newly ordered Yorkshire Woollen District vehicles were borrowed until two further Barnsley cars arrived, along with a track cleaner and snow plough. Rather crude covers were soon fitted to the upper decks, a one man car came from Yorkshire Woollen for use on the lightly used Smithies run in 1905 and a further car new from BET in 1912. This was No.14, the last in the fleet, which soldiered on with proper top covers fitted at £224 apiece in 1922. The little system closed on 31st August 1930, to be replaced by Leyland Titan double deckers over the same routes. Scrapping of the cars took place at the depot in Upper Sheffield road after a modest and honest life of almost thirty years. As the company had now become Yorkshire Traction, their image did not fit the times. In 1913, as Barnsley District, the company had commenced running motor buses to Hoyland, Grimethorpe, Royston, Goldthorpe and Wombwell, using a fleet of ten vehicles. From 1914 a further ten allowed a service to Doncaster via Goldthorpe, but a large faction in the Barnsley District management tended to favour the new 'trackless' tram, most likely the same who, in 1901 had advocated a light railway to Doncaster with branches thrown in.

Four Dearne authorities, Thurnscoe, Wath, Wombwell and Bolton-on-Dearne reached an agreement to implement the above Barnsley & District plans of 1907 and 1911, which would involve the use of trackless trams, and had consulted the Leeds and Bradford authorities who had started to use the new vehicles as early as 24th June 1911, making them pioneers in this rather curious field. Nearer to hand Rotherham had begun in October 1912, supervised by a General Manager who had transferred himself from the Bradford system. It was, however, somewhat perverse of the four councils on the Dearne to apply for a light Railway Order in November 1913, though they may have had an eye on the neighbouring Mexborough & Swinton tramway system; the length of run would be 18¼ miles at a total cost of £150.000. Opened in 1907, in its first year the M & ST ran over a system of stud contacts on the Dolter system, the studs being energised by each tram as it passed over the preceding one. Unfortunately these did not always switch off after use and caused lively street antics on the part of horses in the roadway. The overhead wire soon appeared on the main route which ran from the Toll Bar east of Mexborough, through the town and then dividing, the line south running via Rawmarsh to meet the Rotherham system at the town boundary. The other branch went due west from Mexborough into a no-man's-land of railways, mines and bridges at Manvers Main on Wath road. By 1915 the Dearne District Light Railways Joint Committee had been formed from members of the earlier four local councils, and were authorised to build a more modest 15¼ miles of tramway route from Barnsley to Wath and Thurnscoe, plus a branch to Manvers to link up with the M & S system, and another to join at Swinton for the same purpose. The Minute book runs from 1913 and shows that some business had already taken place before 1915 was reached, in fact a grant of £75,000 had been awarded for improvements in the Dearne District by the Development Commissioners and it was noted that street lighting was to be of greater importance than the provision of a tramway.

On 18th June 1915 when the draft order for the DDLR was announced, there was £2661 4s 2d. in the coffers, with £244 14s. in the lighting fund. There were several objections raised against the new trams at this time, some frivolous and some serious. One of the first was placed by the Dearne Valley Railway Company, owners of a late comer to the railway scene and which passed west-east through halts at Grimethorpe, Goldthorpe and Barnburgh towards Doncaster. They opposed the title of the new system but, in fairness to themselves, did propose the alternative of 'the South Yorkshire Light Railway Company', possibly too pretentious for a mere tramway. At about this time a meeting took place in London at the Regent Palace Hotel, chaired by Mr. Oxley and supported by Messrs. Riley, Probert and Nokes. The omens were not good, however, for the Great War was at hand, casting its sable cloak over every attempt to summon enthusiasm for such puny concerns. No powers were available to construct Railways 13 and 14, as the engineer-in-charge could not accept any responsibility, while the abandonment of Railways Nos. 18 and 19 was accepted. Possibly these numbers would refer to the Darfield branch from Wombwell and a spur round from Manvers to Bolton-on-Dearne, both of which were shown on the original scheme. The Mexborough & Swinton Traction Company had caused a flutter in the dove cote by converting its routes to trackless trams in 1915. This disappointment served, however, to mitigate the unpleasantness encountered in dealings with the Great Central Railway, successors of the MS & L, who absolutely opposed any crossing of their lines on the level by DDLR trams to reach the M & S terminus at Manvers, citing the dual nuisances of special trackwork required and intrusive overhead trolley wiring, which would be a potential aerial hazard. Many places, as Hull, integrated the two quite well, with signals available for both trains and roadway.

In the end the Manvers route from Wath was to become a white elephant, going nowhere of interest and serving few residences, only the collieries and the level crossing, Wath Staith, of ill repute.

Matters were wound down for the duration of wartime, with a Draft Extension & Abandonment Order issued in 1915, following a question in the House of Lords about the feasibility of the tramway system. However, Messrs. Stephen Sellon & Partners were appointed engineers on 18th July 1919, in case difficulties and differences might be resolved. Sleeping Beauty awoke in 1919, as hoped for, to find an Order abandoning the original line to Bolton, as mentioned, and its replacement by a shorter, though more tortuous route from Wath to Bolton, where the line took to a section of reserved track to avoid three stiff turns through the centre of the village. All this was heard at a meeting held with the Light Railway Committee on 17th December 1919, primarily to discuss its future; this was followed by a meeting in Barnsley Town Hall on 21st January 1920 to report findings and sound out any development. What appears surprising is how lukewarm Barnsley appeared to be to the prospect of having a link with the numerous populace on its eastern side. Active opposition, as noted, came from the railways and one particular bone of contention was the extra weight which would be carried by a bridge on the Brampton road spanning the Elsecar railway branch, as well as the Knoll beck and local canal. Cars on the DDLR would all be single deckers due to the low bridges, especially that beneath the MR line at Wath on the Dearne road. Needless to state, the railways had little about which to complain in this instance, as the station was overhead. The diversion at Bolton was ratified on 20th December 1921, removing the line of route from Angel street and Station road and, incidentally from a slice of built-up area as revenue.

No. 6 at the 'Car barns'. Note the gloomy background, the crest on car side and what appears to be the service timetable posted inside the saloon. *Barnsley Libraries*

By 1921 costs had risen to £300,000 and an extension of time for eventual completion was sought. This was granted by the new Minister of Transport with the proviso that all must be completed within three years. It was now becoming a little late and out-of-date to be discussing tramways when the new motor bus and charabanc were appearing more frequently on local and excursion runs, so there were growing misgivings by several local councillors. Still, the area was still an important coal mining one and this crucial fact, that a major employer was involved, won the day. The area already supported a Joint Gas Board, while the Dearne District Electricity Board was yet to be formed, on 1st July 1923. There was also still a hankering after those 'tracklesses'. A deputation of local councillors visited the Ministry of Transport to request more financial assistance for the construction of the line; their efforts, perhaps surprisingly met with success and the line was opened on 12th July 1924.

Prior to the opening, the members of the Committee were:

Wombwell:	Collindridge, Bellshaw, Mellor, Ogden, Thompson, Hallsworth, Preston, Jardine.
Wath:	Robson, Adkins, Braithwaite, Thomson.
Bolton:	Taylor, Probert, Horn.
Thurnscoe:	Nokes, Hazard.

The first Chairman was Mr G H Oxley of Wombwell.

The names of most of the above, including that of Mr. P.M. Walker, solicitor of Messrs. Bury & Walker of Barnsley, representing the DDLR Board and clerk to Wombwell UDC will appear here in the course of the next few pages.

The Dearne District Light Railway is Opened

The opening day was reported with great gusto in 'The South Yorkshire Times' of the day, though not quite so expansively in 'The Barnsley Chronicle', as might well be expected. A procession of twelve cars waited to set off from the Barnsley terminus near the Alhambra to the depot, known as the 'car barns' for some reason, possibly because of the Scottish influences at work within the company. The depot was at the turn on Brampton road, Wombwell. Departure was a little later than the planned time of three pm. The first car was decked with flags and bunting and was driven off by Mr. Mark Nokes, a Thurnscoe man who was Chairman of the DDLR Committee. With him on the platform was Mr. G H Hurst MP. Mr Hallsworth representing Wombwell UDC drove the second car and Mr. Marshall Robson, representing Wath UDC the third. Not to be forgotten the representative of Bolton UDC, Mr. George Probert was in charge of the fourth, the remainder being brought along by the paid staff.

A large crowd was present in Doncaster road to see off the contingent after a bouquet had been presented on behalf of the conductresses by the Misses Hallsworth and Winder, daughters of Wombwell councillors, to Mrs. Coutts, wife of Mr. Fred Coutts, General Manager of the new tramway. All councillors for the four areas involved were present at this happy ceremony.

Over the canal bridge to journey's end *Photo: S.L. Smith*

No. 22 at the Alhambra terminus in Barnsley. *Photo: S.L. Smith*

Progress along the route was slow, as was to be expected, and it was not until 4.15 pm. that the caravan reached the car barns where Mr. Nokes opened the gates and a union flag was hoisted over the site to begin the celebrations.

Mr. Nokes made the first speech, and is quoted below:

He said that he had great pleasure in declaring the DDLR open, and hoped shortly to see it serving the public. It had been a long and weary wait, but they had reached the great day at last. He wanted to take the opportunity of telling the public something of what they had gone through while preparing and carrying through the scheme. When first they came to consider the idea of a transport system for the Dearne Valley, they thought in their simplicity that all they had to do was to run round the district and survey it, declare it suitable and get the trams going. But they soon found out that there was a great deal more in it than that.

They had to hold inquiries in each of the districts to get the ratepayers' consent and then go to the Board of Trade for their powers, encountering at every step of the way the most determined opposition from railways, collieries, canals - every trade and interest in the neighbourhood. It really looked as if nobody wanted the miners to ride about the district at all. However, they managed to convince public opinion at home, and the Government officials who had inquired into their scheme that what they were doing was for the benefit of the district, and they obtained their authority after a long, hard struggle. They had been waiting for ten or eleven years, waiting for the satisfaction they were now enjoying. They had got many of their opponents won over and they felt that they had solid backing of the people behind them. He certainly hoped so. He thought that the people in each of the four districts concerned in the scheme would be determined to ,make it a success. They had the power to do so if they chose. During the last few years the districts had been served by the Barnsley Traction Company and other organised bus services, and he was not going to say that they had not been well served. But these buses had been using the district roads and entailing heavy expenditure on their maintenance without contributing anything to the cost at all. That light railway scheme would give the public the use of their own roads for their own purposes. He was hopeful that not only would the tramway undertaking succeed, but that the bus services, which had done so much to prove the need for a light railway, would co-operate rather than compete with this new enterprise. (Applause)

Mr. Hallsworth then spoke, sounding a more cautious note in reserving his full pleasure at the scheme until a year's time when the first balance sheet would appear. He also drew attention to the fact that already their nearest neighbours had taken up the tram lines and replaced by railless trolley vehicles, drawing the inference that the roads in that part of the world were not likely to wear out much more quickly as a result! M & ST track maintenance had been costing them £9,000 per annum.

At Wombwell the party collected Mr. W. McGibbon, General Manager of the M & ST Company, and Major G.L. Hall of the

Ministry of Transport, who had conducted the customary inspection of the new line on the previous Wednesday without any adverse comments. He expected the system to be running on half service from the following Monday.

The cars left the depot at 6 pm. and ran on to High Street, Wath, where a halt was made at the new power station. Mr. Robson left his driving for a short while to declare the structure open, stating in his speech that, after ten difficult years they were beginning to enjoy the fruits of their labour. The DDLR Committee had borne the brunt of much criticism, especially in Wath, one of the most progressive of small towns, where folk had seen roads widened and buildings removed (as nothing compared with the scene today), and he began to wonder where it would all lead. When the idea of a tramway was mooted eleven years ago, it was considered the easiest matter in the world to provide one until opposition was met from the railways, coal owners, large employers of labour and large rate payers in every one of the districts. In time the colliery companies were persuaded that the tramway would be in their interests and those of the men. The opposition dwindled, though not before £15,000 had been spent in promoting the line instead of the £5,000 planned originally. As for the bus company, it was up to the public to choose by use whether it would be retained or not, otherwise it would be like a man who, having bought a car travelled to work by taxi. Mr. Robson concluded by referring to the inscription on a fishermen's monument at Caistor in Norfolk. 'Men of Caistor never turn back'. It was true that he and his elected Council would never turn back from promoting the DDLR. Mr. Nokes, in reply thanked the speaker and reminded his audience that the latter had always been known as 'the fighting machine from Wath'.

The final stage of what became the main line and probably the most interesting took the cars north to the terminus at Thurnscoe through variegated scenery to a final stop by the side of Houghton lane without the ceremony of any shelter. Here, as at Wath a large throng had gathered and Mr. John Parker, Chairman of Thurnscoe UDC gave a short address in which he stated that his village had probably suffered more from isolation than any of the other places served, but that he hoped that Thurnscoe would benefit from closer contact with the 'near townships'. Certainly he could include Barnsley in his remark, as the competitive motor buses were now bringing the two places within a short time span of each other, closer than the trams would ever achieve.

Messrs, Nokes and Robson had valiantly driven the cars from end to end of the route and would have been eagerly looking forward to the celebration dinner which was held afterwards at the Butcher's Arms in High street. This was given by the engineers and contractors for the committee and others, presided over by the Jack of all Trades Mr. Nokes. Mr. G.H. Hurst, the local MP had a few interesting remarks to offer in his speech, referring to the fact that Darfield would have liked to have been served by the light railway, but lacked the confidence to join in the earlier struggles. He stated that one principal effect of the service provided would be to enable miners to live away from the collieries in which they worked, not on top of them as previously. It is true that certain attractively laid out new estates with semis and gardens did appear, as at Highgate and on the south side of Wath where it was brightest and breeziest.

Nos. 10 and 17 meet the throng in Wombwell.
Rotherham Libraries

No. 3 at speed in Barnsley road Wombwell *Lens of Sutton*

The Mayor of Barnsley, Councillor G.F. Ward wished success to the scheme and said that it would benefit the town and the whole of the mining community. Mr. Probert agreed that miners should live away from the colliery yard and in the fresh air; he looked forward to the cementing of the small Dearne Valley towns into one united whole. The toast 'The Industries of the Dearne Valley' was proposed by Mr. Arthur Neal, one time Parliamentary Secretary to the MOT who delivered, appropriately, a well-turned speech which is worth quoting:

'As we were carried along the route today, I noticed something to which no reference has been made. If this railway is to be financially successful in competition with private enterprise - and I am going to say nothing in favour of either one side or the other - it must be gratifying to the Committee today to see the route lined from end to end with the inhabitants of this district who were beaming their satisfaction. I think that was a most encouraging augury for the success of the undertaking. This railway is carried through a wondrously populated district and I saw, as we went along, such an abundance of youthful citizens that there seems no likelihood of the population falling. (Laughter) I do think that you have every prospect of financial success. You may have to wait a little time for the result, and I would advise you not to be too optimistic and not to be too much discouraged if your earlier returns do not quite meet your expenditure. This new undertaking has to encounter substantial competition and, therefore, if your highest hopes are not immediately realised, do not be unduly depressed. (Hear, hear.) Regarding the industries of the Dearne Valley, they might be summed up in one word - Coal. I do not suppose there is one person present who does not wish well to the mines and the miners, for coal was the one industry upon which all the others depended. It is upon coal that the industrial supremacy of this country has been established, but a great transition is taking place. Other countries are now producing power in the more convenient and portable form of electricity, and I believe that, unless this country takes a great step forward in the direction of developing electrical power from its coal and water supplies, we should be left in the race for competition in the manufacture of goods.'

In other speeches Mr. Braithwaite of Wath said that he regretted that the tram did not reach Barnsley station and that one of their greatest difficulties would be in getting the public to come from the centre of town to Doncaster road end, but he hoped that Barnsley would assist in 'getting the trams through'. As time showed, they had other interests and ideas about the trams. Alderman S. Jones replied for Barnsley and said en passant that the DDLR would be up against one of the finest bus services in the country who were not going to be beaten if they could help it. He was sure, however, that the tramways could be utilised as well as for carrying of passengers and that a service during the night could be used to the common good. This final remark rings like a class instance of damnation with faint praise!

Local menfolk watch No. 17 pass in High Street Wombwell

Lens of Sutton

The Line's Construction and Route

The Consolidated Construction Company were to build the line and install the equipment. The system was similar to that in general use at the time, essentially single track basically, with a double run of overhead wiring, one line for each direction which provided continuity and would obviate the need for pointwork overhead at passing loops. It is assumed that facing track points were changed by removable hand lever, unless sprung at each end of the loop for the correct direction of travel. Work began at the Thurnscoe end in May 1923 and was reported to be well under way a year later. A late deviation was called for along Burman road in Wath to serve a new council estate and, incidentally, saving the cost of a new road. An Amendment Order was applied for and authorised on 24th June 1924. Test and training runs were carried out during June before the official inspection of just over 14 miles of track, nearly all of which was single, apart from some 3.8 miles. Total mileage authorised had been 15.11 miles; the total cost was £279,215 of which £274,142 was borrowed.

General view of the 'Car Barns' depot, with a review of four cars and the repair vehicle on the left. Rotherham Libraries

No. 25 ready to return to the Woodman Inn, probably in West Melton. *Photo: S.L. Smith*

The Opening Day was 14th July 1924, excepting the run from Wath to the Woodman Inn at Swinton which could not be in action until September, due to the deviation above.

The first chairman was Mark Nokes, with administration by the Light Railway Joint Committee. The clerk of Bolton UDC was Clerk to the Committee and also, for good measure to the Electricity Board. The Head Office and Depot were at Wombwell, where the General Manager and staff were based. As already mentioned, the power for the line was generated at Wath. The standard gauge track was well laid on railway sleepers buried in the roadway, while the cars were slightly superior in that they were driven by 'motormen' and supervised almost exclusively by conductresses. A bone of contention was the inability to link up the wires and rails with the Barnsley system in Doncaster road; things abutted here but did not permit running powers, a point which seems odd today, though it is fairly certain that Barnsley knew that its own system had not much longer to survive. The independent bus companies shared the same terminus outside the Alhambra.

At the Woodman Inn, also known locally as 'Woodman's Inn', the DDLR made a fine double Y junction with the M & ST facing south towards Rotherham, a facility which, ironically, was hardly ever used.

To describe the route now, beginning at the Barnsley end and taking the terminus to the Stairfoot curve as the first section. The run was quite undulating, firstly down to the 'Pindar Oaks', followed by an ascent past the Kendray hospital, then over the top and down beneath the Midland line overbridge to the sharp right hand bend at Stairfoot where the line doubled for the duration of the curve, as the line came up against the large and impressive overbridge which spanned the road junction proper where the Cudworth road departed up its own steep hill. On this section there was a run-round at the Alhambra terminus and passing places at Gold street, Cemetery road, Wall street, Masborough Hill, Lambert road, just below the first railway bridge, the next school and finally the long, double stretch at Stairfoot. All passing places would be in view of the next point ahead, except of course in thick fog. Once round the bend and the line took on an easterly, flatter route, through collieries, brickyards and sundry factories towards Wombwell, with, firstly, a passing place at the Keel Inn followed by one serving the brickyard. Beyond this was a fairish run to the next, then further on to a longish stretch of double track crossed by Aldham railway bridge, a low one which carried the incessant, thundering coal trains from Wath marshalling yard up the steep Wentworth bank, a banking engine bringing up the rear.

Two more loops, at the Aldham Glass Bottle Works and the Halfway House and we have reached the outskirts of Wombwell, a busy little town made even more so by the double track of the tramway through the centre and across the market place, to be followed by a short single section, then more double near the schools and old Wombwell Hall. On the outward run the Town Hall was the fare stage (4 miles), while the Empire Theatre did the honours in the other direction, providing a goodly fount of traffic on Saturday nights for the DDLR and motor buses. Next along the line of route came Tunstall Cross, where crossroads served Broomhill and Jump. To the south lay the housing estate built for the DDLR employees off Lundhill road, with the more splendid structures facing the latter and the humdrum on Ewden and Broomhead roads which ran east towards the depot land behind. One can easily query the notion of having all one's staff neatly housed in a single area alongside the place of work, though it was marvellously convenient for operating purposes with staff as 'sitting targets' for a spot of quick relief. However, the whole principle did run counter to one of the stated purposes of having such a tramway to start with, that of the worker being allowed to live away from his or her daily occupation. The daily frustration of what could well be a stifling atmosphere where everybody lived and breathed the same topic and knew each other's business can easily be imagined.

No. 22 about to take a sharp corner at West Melton.

Rotherham Libraries

No. 5 passes a horse and cart in Wath

Rotherham Libraries

It was a short run to the Junction Inn (the Guide Post) where the Wath road and Brampton roads divided. A passing place was here also, before the trams turned into the latter road and met the triangle of points and wiring into the depot, giving access from both directions, from which two sets of three parallel lines led into the sheds. Passing loops were thick on the ground hereabouts along a decent stretch of straight road through the large estate at Brampton. First came the loop on top of the Dearne & Dove canal bridge, then the next by the aptly named Concrete cottages, of seven ranks on the south side, the point where a short working of the service for nearby Cortonwood colliery turned round, then along Knoll Beck lane to the lower edge of the estate mentioned earlier to a loop by the miners' recreation ground at the Bull's Head. A short way up the hill came an extended passing loop at the Brampton Bierlow schools, round which the road passed; this was somewhat difficult to sight correctly from the previous stop, but could be achieved with practice. One wonders how many motormen carried binoculars! On the Brampton road was a short passing loop again, before the turn at Christ church into the road to West Melton, which had a short run of double track probably more for neatness at an intersection to keep the trams on the logical side of the road directionwise, rather than for operating purposes. The line now ran downhill through West Melton towards Wath, with a passing loop at Oak Lea avenue, where the new estate lay, then downwards to meet the lower Barnsley road from Hollowgate, at which point was a sharp curve in the narrow street, followed by a considerable stretch of double track into Wath proper. The two branches, to be met with anon, would terminate here, while the principal halts were the Cosy Cafe, and Picture House, shared with two local bus firms and a Yorkshire Traction Saturday service. Mr. Denton explains some of the working arrangements in his own book on the DDLR:-

'When cars reversed here, motormen commonly released the hand wheel brake completely at the driving end, which allowed the car to roll under its own momentum down the slight gradient and coast over the facing points on to the other line. Meanwhile, with his controller locking key in his hand, the motorman had walked through the car to the other, new driving end just in time to re-apply the hand brake and park the car to await time. While this was happening, the conductress had pulled down the trolley boom to right angles, waited patiently whilst the car coasted past and then replaced the boom on the wires, all with the minimum of movement. Time and labour studies are supposed to be something modern'. The author does not think that this sort of carry-on would cut much ice in today's climate of heavy traffic and preoccupation with the safety of the individual.

West street in Wath was single line, due to narrowness, before a long section of double track began at the Town Hall, to run round the curve of Mongomery road bringing the traveller to the hub of things at Sandygate, where was situated the Majestic Theatre. Sandygate ran south to Mexborough on the A633 and would have taken the tramway branch to the Woodman Inn, had not a decision been taken to keep a little further with the main route along the High Street and turn off later up Burman road to take in the new estate. Once Wath had been left behind, the tramway was now in the wilds and returned to single track as far as Bolton canal bridge, over which the main route turned to run on to distant Thurnscoe, with a branch running straight on along Wath road to Manvers with the sole passing loop at the schools at Gore Hill before terminating a little further on. The junctions in Wath were not symmetrical, the north one leaving first followed by the south one a little further along.

On the Woodman branch was a longish stretch of double track at the south end of Burman road taking it into Sandygate, then there were two further passing places, one of them at Quarry Hill before the arrival at Woodman Inn where track and wiring were laid into the M & ST system southwards.The DDLR car would wait time on the curve towards Rotherham.

The main line towards Thurnscoe from Wath had quite a lively, if rather lonely run to Bolton-on-Dearne, passing close to three railway stations in the initial stages. First it crossed the GC line to Barnsley with its commodious station on the right hand side, then ran down the bridge slope to discover the tidy little H & B station in a coal yard on the left, and lastly running beneath the Midland main line to Leeds by a narrow stone bridge arch 10 ft. 6 ins high to cope with a tram vehicle which was ten foot in height before the overhead trolley arm was depressed to the side to allow passage. The actual station here was on the bridge itself and, surprisingly, no passing loop was provided near here for the trams and any potential customers. The next lay some distance further on near a minor meander of the Dearne just before Upper Mill which ran from the power of the river proper just beyond.

The run in to Bolton now lay uphill along a straight road with a long line of terrace houses as far as the junction with the Wath road at the top. Turning right here, one found a passing loop and, shortly beyond, the cars turned north east to enter the only section of reserved track on the system which crossed, firstly, a road to Thurnscoe via Highgate and then passed along a hedged corridor, keeping a small quarry to the west side. Station road was then reached and the fare stage at the Collingwood Hotel. There was a turn due north into Furlong road and next a passing place, the other of only two in the village. The line was diverted from the original plan to reserved track to avoid nasty turns at the end of Wath road, High street and Station road. In the event the cars passed round the small Ladycroft housing estate which was built for the local railway workers - the S & K station was a little way off to the east. The reserved section of track was controlled by light signals which, if similar to those in operation on a comparable section of the Burton & Ashby system would be red/green, though a simple on/off would be just as effective. Presumably the lights would be in use here, not because of the reserved section but because of the length, as trams would have to wait at each end of the village in the passing places. It is interesting that the two previous sections must have been of similar or even greater length to work, and yet they seemed to survive without light indicators.

No. 30 swings round the curve at Montgomery Road, Wath, passing a Yorkshire Traction bus and a fine gathering of local folk.
Lens of Sutton

No. 30 climbs Burman Road in Wath on the Woodman service, past a miniscule petrol vehicle. Rotherham Libraries

Furlong road ran north beneath the York-Swinton railway line for a good distance to reach the passing place serving the model housing estate which was part of Bolton-on-Dearne, before turning into Goldthorpe road at the Green where there was a spacious park with band stand, sports ground, cycle track, bowling and tennis equipment. The road curved round all these blandishments to reach a passing loop at the Buxton Arms, north of which the line made a dog's leg into Goldthorpe High street, then north again through the built-up area of a quite neatly planned little town, over the Dearne Valley Railway from Wakefield to Doncaster (Edlington) - really this was the L & Y by another name - and then sharp left into Barnsley road to another passing place shared by not one, but two Picture Theatres, each on the north side of the road. Centrally placed, this would be the focal point of Goldthorpe and be very busy at times. Capriciously now, the trams went westwards to the Halfway Hotel, passing over three different railway lines, the H & B, DVR (again), and S & K en route. Of the three, only the DVR could field anything remotely like a station, this being a tatty old coach body dumped at the side of the line, ready fodder for vandals, its access along a cinder track through a coal depot. However, it was quite close to the last mentioned tram stop.

From here came a rural ride as the car swung sharply north again along Nicholas lane, past the school and this time beneath the DVR and, a little further on, beneath the bridge carrying the spur line from the DVR round to the north east and the S & K line. Just north of here was the most countrified of passing places, set in a twist of the road and with no habitation in view; possibly this was a sop to the owner of Thurnscoe Hall, whose rear entrance, a good $^{1}/_{4}$ miles away along a drive was to be found beyond the trees. The line may have started with a bang but it ended with a whimper in that there was to be one further crossing place, at Garden street, before the line ran on along Houghton road, westwards again to end at Chapel street, with fields on the north side after schools and Thurnscoe park behind the new housing. The end of the line was designated as the Thurnscoe Hotel and the presence of the trams encouraged the development of a new estate around Merrill road on the north side. In some respects it was a pity that the line did not, instead, turn right at the top of Shepherd lane into Station road and terminate by the Station Hotel, which would have served a vast housing area at Thurnscoe East, as well as being of use to many of the miners at Hickleton colliery. However, the planners were more than likely foiled by the presence of two adjacent and parallel railway overbridges across Station road which would prove to be too low to negotiate.

Something which really should not be stated here is that the direct route by bus to Barnsley had been in being for ten years before the trams arrived, was half the distance and quicker to boot! On a bad day the end-to-end journey could take $1^{1}/_{2}$ hours.

The Rolling Stock

The thirty cars used on the system were constructed by Messrs. Dick, Kerr of Preston, now part of GEC, and delivered by rail to Wombwell MR station yard, from where they were carted down Hough lane to the depot on Brampton road. Nos.1-25 came first, bodies and trucks separately; these were assembled by the firm's engineers at the depot. Nos. 26-30 were ordered when the Woodman Inn branch was authorised. A similar manoeuvre had taken place many years before at Doncaster when that corporation's trams had been shipped in by rail, this time, however, with the top deck (they had two) removed for convenience.

The DDLR cars were specially designed for the line, longer than normal at 32 ft. but with the standard features of angular dash, corner posts with two vertical mouldings and roof which was almost flat and squared at the ends. There were five large windows to each side fitted with sham curtains, each with two top lights and hinged openings. The centre front window could be hinged upwards, handy for a blow in summer and to deal with fogs in winter. Seating within was longitudinal, for 36 passengers. Mr Massingham of Wombwell writes to say 'Some of the lattice seats eventually appeared in the surgery waiting rooms of doctors Jardine and Etches, to add to any tension felt by any visit.'

Peckham P22 8ft. 6in. wheelbase trucks were fitted with two 40hp. motors. The driving platforms at each end were somewhat cramped to fit in as much seating capacity as possible, the motorman sharing the space with a large vertical wheel used to work the hand brake. The platforms were open to either side for quick entry and exit, though the front offside entry to the saloon and saloon door were always locked when the car was running. A large headlamp adorned the centre of each end below the number, while the company crest was sported down the centre of each car side. Destination blinds were mounted in boxes on the roof at the ends. Livery was maroon and cream, the undergear also being maroon; lining was in gold.

There is a date for this shot 15/8/29 as D.D.L.R. car stands at Woodman Inn to return. The photographer's bike bell is just visible in the bottom corner. *S.L. Smith*

No record of any accident has been mentioned officially anywhere, and the cars were in good condition when closure took place after only nine years of service, with the result that nine cars were able to be sold, Nos. 11,12,17,18 and 19 to Falkirk, where, unfortunately each had to be shortened by half a window at the outer end of each side due to clearance problems. The other four (unrecorded) went to Lytham St. Anne's, becoming Nos. 51-54 and unaltered, these lasting there until 1937 in a rather flash livery of blue and white. They were restricted in use to Lytham proper, as Blackpool would not permit the 'foreigners' to stray on to their own system.

Mr. L. Green has unearthed a picture of one of the car bodies, heavily reduced and in use as a shed in the Sheffield area.Two of the cars also did duty as store sheds at Stairfoot

Brickworks; who knows, perhaps other survivors may yet turn up.

Bell communication was by a leather strap along the inside of the saloon overhead on each side. Doncaster trolleybuses seemed to make do with long lengths of string in the early days, while current East Yorkshire bus practice has a bell strip down each side of the bus which never works. With the longitudinal seating there was plenty of room for standing passengers who had time enough to read the adverts, a timetable sheet or an exhortation such as 'passengers entering or leaving the car whilst in motion (the car) do so at their own risk.' No dogs were allowed. Attempts were made to heat the cars from the power available, but these were dropped without any noticeable success. A trial with snow plough was also a failure. The long trolley arms were controlled by retriever wires attached to a spring driven drum which could be detached and taken round to the correct end of the tram by the conductress when in use. This was a modern device, several years ahead of its time, before it was adapted for use in Hull before 1939 for the corporation's trolleybuses.

The depot was equipped with six roads for standage, each holding five cars and with two roads extending into a maintenance area. Outside,the entry lines, as seen above, formed a triangle which could be used for turning purposes if necessary, while the whole site was securely contained by a high fence and lockable gates. At most only 14 cars were in normal daily use leaving a considerable number under-employed in the depot. The vehicles were a good 'buy', solidly built and quite modern-looking for the period, compared with the motor buses. Appropriate entries/exits could be shut off by lattice gates if necessary, so that a car might be operated as a one-manner.

Any running emergencies were dealt with by a tower wagon and its crew manned in two shifts. A Leyland was acquired new for the task in 1928 and painted in DDLR livery.

Another 'Special Car', No. 21 again, passed at the low arch beneath the Midland main line. No shortage of admirers.

Rorhterham Libraries

Operational Staff

It must be remembered that the whole DDLR concept was the modification of a very early plan set out in 1901, with a longer route between Barnsley and Thurnscoe taking in Manvers Main, then round to Bolton with a strong hint of through working over the M & ST to Denaby and Conisbrough and, dare it be mentioned, over a possible link to Warmsworth on the Doncaster system. However, it was not to be, neither was the more probable branch to Darfield from Wombwell. In the final event the parts proved to be stronger than the whole, with many more passengers making use of shorter links than those who might choose to travel through from end to end - presumably very few. At every turn of course the motor bus was in constant competition. As in other places such as Doncaster, the cars did not start until after lunch on Sundays, but on weekdays first off the mark was the 4.15 am. from Cortonwood lane end to take the miners to Barnsley. This service formed the first of the through runs during the day at 15-30 minutes headway. A car would need up to three hours for the round trip, with timed thirty minutes stages between Barnsley and Wombwell,Wombwell and Wath MR station and a final stage to Thurnscoe. A trial was made in running some through services between Barnsley and the Woodman Inn for variety, as well as a Saturday service between the Woodman Inn and Barnsley in the afternoon, but with little success. Normally one car only was in service on each of the branches giving a half hourly service with the cars terminating at West Melton. At the main time of day eleven or twelve cars would be in use on the through service.

Timetables did exist and were to be found at the roadside stops, but unfortunately nothing has come into the author's possession as yet, nor have any tickets.

Mr. A.S. Denton's booklet on the tramway system, published in 1980, offers some interesting extra details. The fares tariff was based on twenty two stages from end to end, and two stages each on the branches, though one wonders how more than one could have been fitted in on the Manvers run. The journeys were by no means a penny a stage, but were better value if one travelled further; children rated half fare and twelve journey tickets were available and allowed an extra ride free. Three stages were charged at 2d, five at 3d. eight at 4d, ten at 5d and thirteen at 6d. Fifteen were charged at 7d, eighteen at 8d, twenty at 9d and end-to-end at 10d. Tickets were of standard pattern of the period, lengthy with stages printed on and coloured to value and use. They were carried by the conductresses in long hand racks and were punched by a bell punch on being issued. Each conductress had her own two letter ticket code, by which tickets issued could easily be checked against the waybill of the issuer. In addition to managing the public affairs on board the tram, the conductress, as mentioned, had to supervise the handling of the re-wiring of the overhead trolley arm as necessary at a terminal point. Under tension the arm could present problems for ladies of slight build and the motorman would have to keep an eye open for any embarrassing difficulties!

No. 21 halts in Bolton cutting. The indicator blind says 'Special Car' so that this could be an opening run. Rotherham Libraries

No. 13 hurries along between Thurnscoe and Goldthorpe
Barnsley Libraries

There was never much need to rush about, even with the powerful motors which could reach roads speeds of ten mph. or more. This was often done and drivers were known to be quite adept at performing fast passing movements through loops by taking the points at speed without stopping. Similarly, cars could be brought to a stand within their own length by a quick return of the control handle from full speed. Points at the passing loop would be spring loaded in favour of the left hand road, so that each car would leave a passing loop against the spring action of the further point and, if reversing, would take the left hand route and thus always be on the correct side of the roadway. Points at the branch junctions in Wath and for serving the depot at Wombwell would be worked by a point iron inserted into the mechanism, while the overhead points would be worked by a stirrup pull on the nearest roadside post.

The far end. Thurnscoe Terminus which ran out away from the camera in front of the new row of shops. *Barnsley Libraries*

The trickiest gradient was the Stairfoot bank down to the railway bridge and a blind corner; trams would have to pause at the top for a partial application of hand and track brakes before proceeding slowly. Fog brought its own troubles, though as the trams had their own track, they had an advantage over other road users. Drivers were able to 'listen in' at a nearby supporting post to hear whether a car in front was on its way into the loop ahead, the swish betraying its location. How progress along single track tram routes was organised was always something of a mystery, the only obvious scheme seeming to be to give priority of progression to one direction along the route. Thus, all cars travelling out of Barnsley could always proceed if the next loop ahead was empty, or if an inbound car was seen to be waiting. Conversely, inbound cars could always wait until the arrival in the loop ahead of the outbound car. This would be most important in the case of the longer single line stretches and any meeting of cars would either necessitate one of them having to back up or an unlikely swap of crew and passengers to allow the journey to be completed. Something similar to the above conjecture must have happened in extreme cases and was essential in bad weather and after dark. Two natural hazards affected the running of the system, the first being subsidence, as on Kendray Hill, Barnsley, where the track and sleepers rose up to seven feet in the air. The second, flooding; in both cases beneath railway bridges at Aldham and in the dip beneath the Midland line arch on Dearne road at Wath.

In the first year of operation 475,876 miles were run by the DDLR, and 2,526,279 passengers were carried, paying a total of £23,000. Working costs were almost £20,000 and repayment of debts. £4,700 which, when added together did not reveal a pleasant picture. Local rates had to rise to defray costs and the motor buses had to levy an extra penny on each of their own fares to give an advantage to the trams. However, it seemed as if a perky and enterprising system was not to survive.

A staff photograph posed outside the Wombwell depot shows roughly a hundred people, which would be approximately the total staff on the books of the DDLR. The local area could provide much female labour and it was decided that conductresses should be employed, as they had already appeared on the Traction single deck motor buses. They were keen and efficient in their duties. It was, however, hard to find employees who were male in an area of full employment in the mining industry; however, the Paisley & District Electric Tramways had just been taken over by Glasgow Corporation Tramways and there were many experienced men who were willing to find a new life in the south. The first General Manager was Major Fred. Coutts who soon went on to Wakefield to the tramway there, leaving his son Ronald to take over the reins. Both the Accountant and Traffic Superintendent came from Paisley, also the Electrician Bill Johnson, his son who manned the tower wagon and his daughter Polly who dealt with ticket records. The turner/fitter and a joiner also came south and joined the new staff. The Wath power station was manned by three DDLR staff.

Outside inspectors were two, Messrs, Sewall and Tweedie. Several of the motormen were Scotsmen, with a rollcall of names sounding like the Gordon Highlanders. From nearer home came other men from Bristol, Sheffield and Bradford.

Uniform was a striking one of green with red piping and brass buttons which had to be cleaned regularly. A long coat, jacket and trousers and peaked cap were worn, the coats being of two weights for summer and winter. The Traction conductresses, by the way, wore brown uniforms.

The Final Days

Ultimately the DDLR was faced with the choice of either reaching a working agreement with its competitors, the Yorkshire Traction Company or selling out to it; beforehand it carried out the customary pattern of activities often found with concerns which are about to give up the ghost - the rash of fresh building, the new signboards or painting of fencing which takes place just before the end arrives. In 1928 the decision was taken to reduce fares, bringing the maximum fare paid on the system over any distance to just 3d., an excellent bargain which brought along more passengers and extra cars in service for a time. However, this was too good to be true and normality had to be resumed very soon. Losses continued to accrue, chiefly due to local competition, almost all of which had its own financial reserves which could tide affairs over, unlike the DDLR. As mentioned twelve journey tickets were introduced at the cost of eleven, similar to Doncaster where unlimited travel on a given route was offered for 2/6d or 2/-, later

No. 10 at the Thurnscoe terminus 7/5/1931. This view would be in the distance in the previous photograph. *Photo S.L. Smith*

A poor and rare shot of an ex D.D.L.R. car running at Lytham St Annes . No. 52 in blue and white livery, seen after having escaped to Blackpool at Gynn Square. *Photo: Dr H.A. Whitcombe*

being for 24 journeys marked off round the card at the same price and terms. With the DDLR a 'support your trams' movement was set up, whereby passengers could buy into a scheme for a small fee entitling them to a green membership card and printed details of services and times of first and last cars, etc. Apart from the dubious distinction of belonging to a sort of club, there was neither financial gain nor privilege in the scheme, the money charged was used to defray printing costs and the idea lapsed due to lack of appeal.

Street scene. An ex D.D.L.R. car gets away from native car No. 1 in Falkirk. *Falkirk Museums*

What might have been an exciting new development was tried in 1928 when M & S double deck trams worked through to Wath and West Melton from Rotherham for a time over the DDLR via Woodman Inn, DDLR crews manning the slow and noisy beasts with their archaic gadgetry, much older than the single decker cars of course. The latter were too long to cope with the vagaries of 'foreign' trackwork. The trials were defeated by poor publicity, single line and slow speeds and were called off in the end when the M & S trams were replaced by Garratt trolleybuses. It was of course possible to travel to Sheffield by tram from Barnsley to Sheffield by changing on to three different systems, though at the cost of much lost time. The M & ST trolleybuses were faster and comfortable when they arrived on the scene and put the DDLR cars to shame. Motorbuses began to choke the routes more and more, preventing any chance of improving tram speeds.

Homemade shortening and adaptation of one of the D.D.L.R. cars purchased by Falkirk. Transverse seating was also fitted.
Falkirk Museums

A final way to passengers' hearts was through their comfort, and No.30 was given improvements thought necessary in the depot workshops while it was off the road for a time, appearing with overhauled gear and new paint and varnish, together with hand grips on the large hand brake wheels fore and aft. Inside the saloon the longitudinal seats had been cut back to four places on each side at one end and three each side at the other for the soiled toilers, while the intervening space was filled with transverse seating with cushions in flowered moquette. The walls were painted white and the lighting was improved, largely through the removal of the old shades. Needless to say the improved car was a success all round. After this there followed the refurbishment of Nos. 29, 28 and 27, the first having brown rexine seating instead of flowery material. No.26 was also lined up for beauty treatment but policy changed before this could be carried out. It will be noted that the cars chosen were of the last batch to appear at Wombwell; apparently the first lot could not be altered because some difference in the position of the sanding boxes.

In April 1929 there was a pooling agreement set up between light railway representatives and BET who had, of course, a large share in the interest of Yorkshire Traction. Here the mileage to be run by each party was agreed, and revenues were collected and distributed equally. Initially there was a drive, reminiscent of previous times, to bring trolleybuses on to DDLR routes and thus enable through running to Rotherham to become reality; however, Barnsley Council, which was now losing its own trams to the motorbus, objected to this and the Bill was thrown out. Instead, a more successful option was promoted in 1930 by Barnsley, therein persuading the DDLR to sell out to Yorkshire Traction for £75,000, or less than half of its original cost. The company would provide buses and pay £3,000 per annum to the Dearne authorities, or half the profits which the buses provided if greater for the first five years, and £2,000 per annum thereafter. Replacement by buses took place on 30th September 1933, without any ceremony. The staff went their various ways; the General Manager, Mr. R. Coutts became Traffic Manager of Yorkshire Traction, while some motormen became bus drivers. Some returned to Paisley, while others joined the Bradford system along with the usable overhead wiring.

Thus ended nine interesting and often quite hectic years which began hard enough in a period of post-war gloom and ended in the throes of the Depression, a bright star in the transport firmament championed by doggedly determined men.

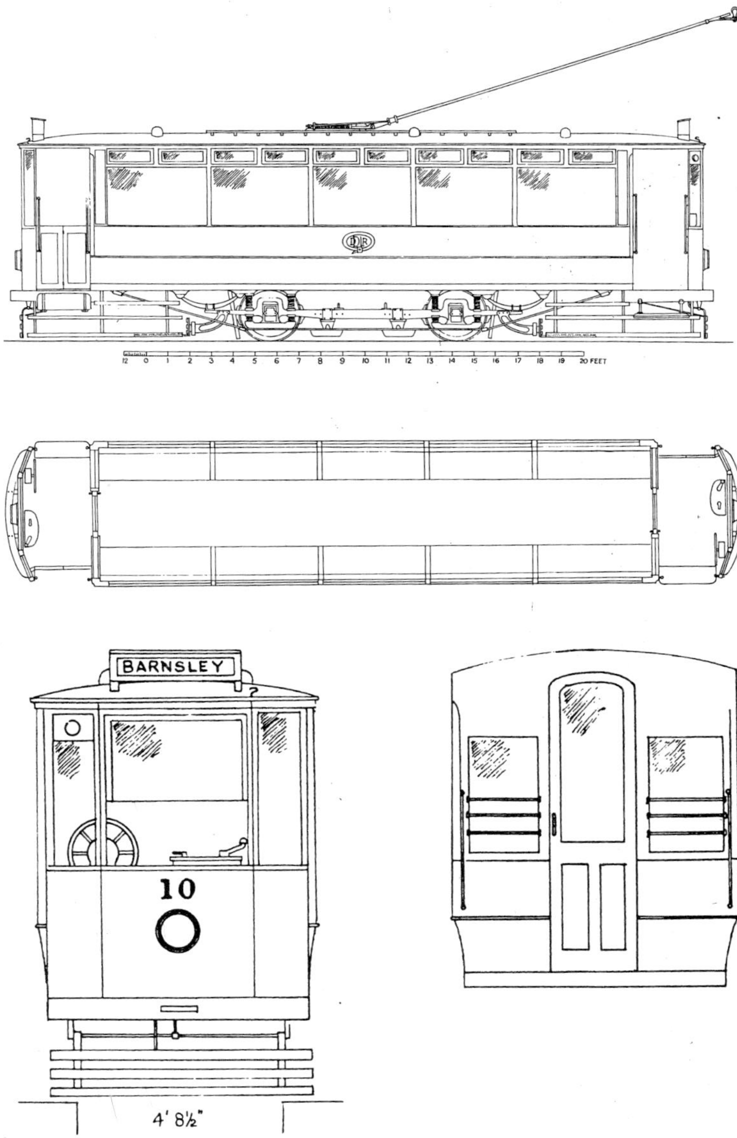

Courtesy: R.W. Rush

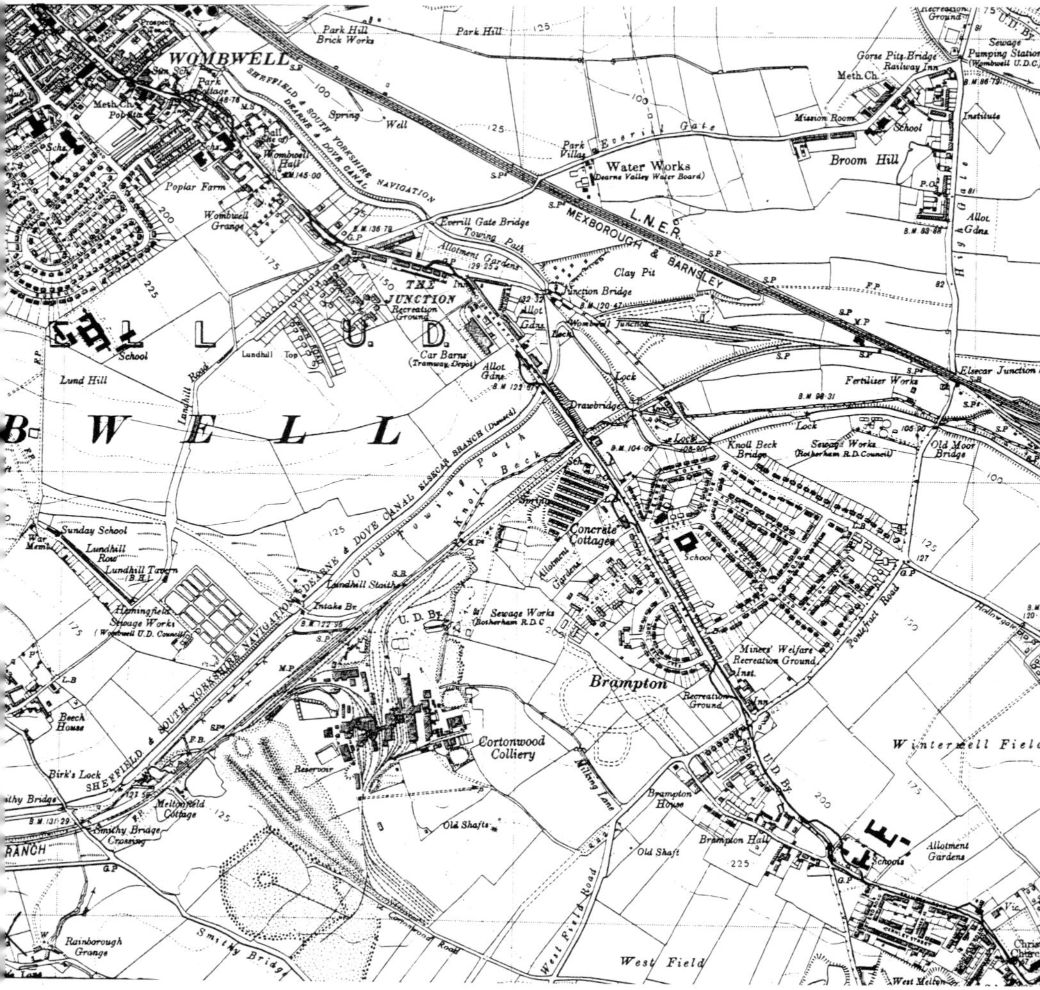

The following three 6 inch maps each mark the route of the tramway, the passing loops being discernable with good sight or a magnifying glass!

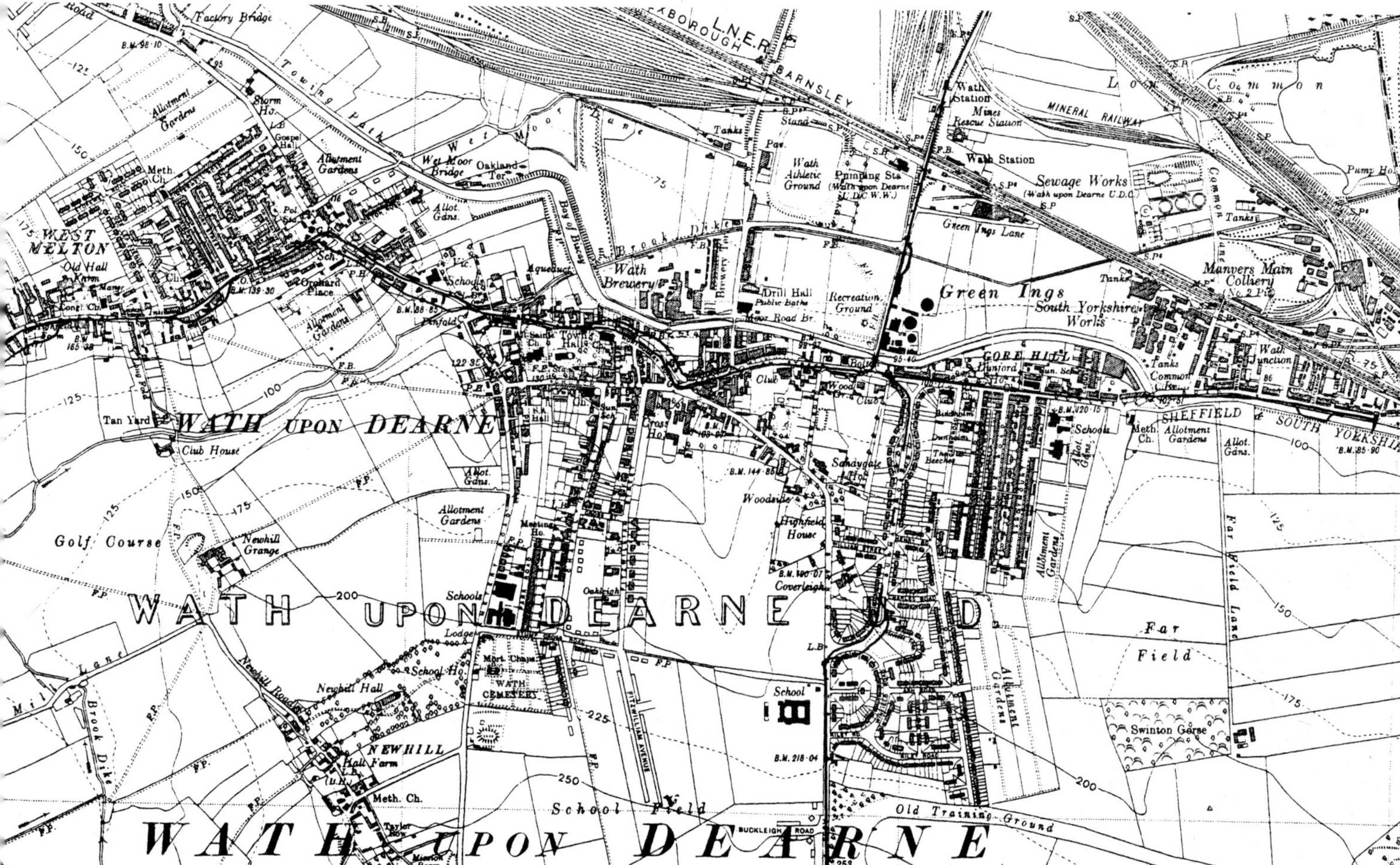
WATH UPON DEARNE
WATH UPON DEARNE U.D.
WEST MELTON
NEWHILL
Green Ings
South Yorkshire Works
Manvers Main Colliery
Wath Station
Mines Rescue Station
Sewage Works
Common Lane
MINERAL RAILWAY
L.N.E.R.
BARNSLEY
Factory Bridge
Towing Path
Wet Moor Lane
Wet Moor Bridge
Oakland Ter.
Bay of Biscay
Brook Dike
Wath Brewery
Wath Athletic Ground
Pumping Sta
Drill Hall
Recreation Ground
Green Ings Lane
Gore Hill
Wath Junction
SHEFFIELD & SOUTH YORKSHIRE
Allotment Gardens
Golf Course
Newhill Grange
Club House
Tan Yard
Newhill Hall
Newhill Road
Hall Farm
Meth. Ch.
Mill Lane
Wath Cemetery
Fitzwilliam Avenue
School Field
Buckleigh Road
Old Training Ground
Far Field
Far Field Lane
Swinton Gorse
Highfield House
Coverleigh
Woodside
Sandygate
Schools
Orchard Place
Penfold
Aqueduct
Storm Ho.
Gospel Hall
Old Hall Farm

THURNSCOE
Recreation Ground
Cricket Ground
Pavilion
Sports Ground
Football Ground
Hall
PARK
War Memt
Misn. Hall
Sun. Sch.
Lodge
CEMETERY
Allotment Gardens
Spiritualist Church
Allot. Gdns.
Hall Farm
Thurnscoe Hall
Allot. Gdns.
Baths
Inst.
Hall
Meth. Ch.
LONDON MIDLAND & SCOTTISH & LONDON & NORTH EASTERN JOINT RAILWAY
L.M.S.R.
HICKLETON COLLIERY BRANCH
WATH BRANCH
N.E.R.
DEARNE VALLEY RAILWAY
Thurnscoe Junction
U. D. By.
Thurnscoe Bridge Lane
Nicholas Lane
Highgate Colliery
Allotment Gardens
R.C. Church
Presby.
Vic.
Church
Halt
Coal Depot
Inst.
School
Misn. Ch.
Allot. Gdns.
Club
Schools
P.O.
Congl. Ch.
Holly Grove
Tank
Highgate House
HIGHGATE
Allot. Gdns.
Hall
Buston Arms Hotel (P.H.)
Welfare Hall
Sports Ground
Highgate Lane
ON UPON DEARNE
BOLTON UPON DEARNE
Goldthorpe Green
Allotment Gardens
Barnsley 7
Doncaster 8
Goldthorpe Brick Works (Disused)

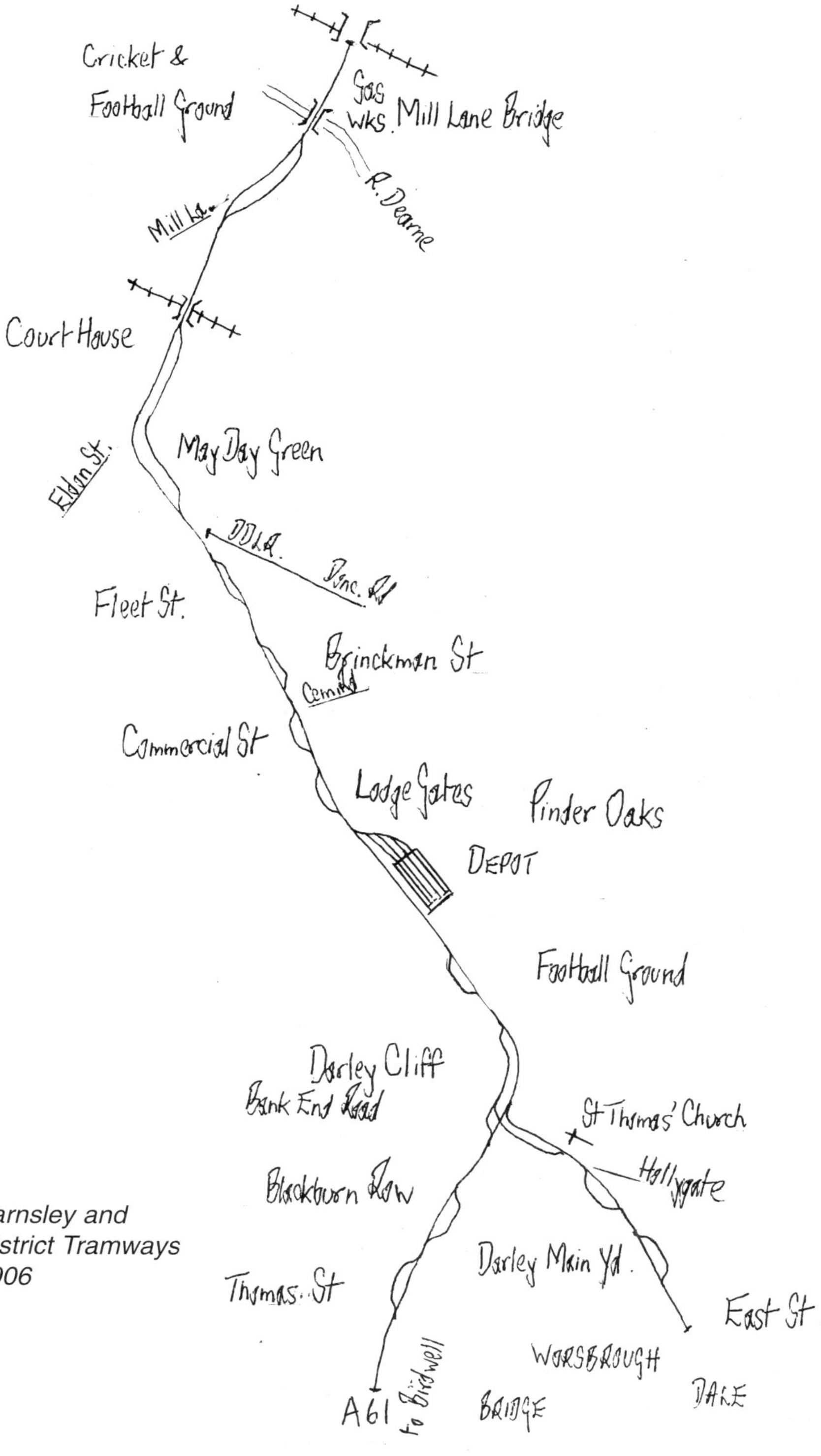

Barnsley and District Tramways 1906

Below is part of the report which appeared in 'The South Yorkshire Times' on Friday, 29th September 1933:-

'The Dearne District Light Railway has come to the end of its career. As from tomorrow it will cease to operate. The system is now to be scrapped and the YTC are to substitute buses. Henceforward no trams will be seen between Thurnscoe and Barnsley, and as soon as practicable the rails will be removed. Apart from financial considerations, there are many who object to trams on principal. Road users who have been harassed and restricted by the operation of trams on this busy route will hold the view that the district is 'well rid'. Not sufficient love has been lost on the trams to make them a paying proposition and therefore no tears will be shed at their obituary. Unfortunately it remains with posterity to pay.

Four local authorities will have from the first five years half profits of the buses running over the tramways routes, or £3,000 per annum, whichever is greater. If the profits are £2,000, then the local authorities receive £2,000, if they are £5,000, they will receive £3,000. If the net profits exceed £6,000, the authorities will receive half. Plans for the disposal of the assets of the DDLR are well advanced. It is believed that one person has offered a price for the whole fleet of trams with the intention of using them for seaside bungalows. Next to the cars the overhead equipment is probably the most valuable among the assets. There should also be a good saleable value in the power station on the main road at Wath.

The Light Railway Committee are the owners of some thirty houses in Landhill lane, Wombwell, erected for the accommodation of the work force. They are substantially built, attractively planned and well preserved. It had been suggested that they could be of special value to the Wombwell UDC, in connection with any possible slum clearance scheme. The taking up of the track and disposal of the steel rails is provided for in an arrangement with the road authorities as a set off. The YTC are to use the car barns at Wombwell as a bus depot, and are filling in the tramcar pits and installing a tank of 10,000 gallons for petrol, the same size as that at the central depot in Barnsley. Thirty buses will be based there and it will be a converging point of Dearne valley traffic. This should be a good thing for enterprise in Wombwell. Most conductresses have been taken on by the YTC, who have also been giving free driving tuition to the tramway's motormen, with a view to widening their field of employability.

All the penny stages at present in operation on the DDLR will be retained and there will be no increase in fares. The protection fare in favour of the light railway would, of course, go by the board. Weekly workmen's tickets would be withdrawn, but daily returns would be available at exactly the same rates and over the same stages. Workmen would be able to pay each day and not pay out 2/6d. in advance. The Wombwell-Barnsley return would remain at 5d. There would be a better service than the current one of ten minutes, with a five minute headway on Saturdays. A spokesman, Mr. G. W. Robinson said:

'We have adopted the whole of the tramsway stage points, but we give our passengers the added advantage of conveying them to our station in Eldon St. This will obviate the danger of congestion at the Alhambra where the traffic in and out of Barnsley has been seriously impeded.'

Definitely the tramway system will be closed down tomorrow night. The last car to run in will come from the Thurnscoe district and there will be no ceremony; it is possible that there will be people with a sentimental desire to travel on the 'last tram'.

M&ST No. 29 at Manvers Terminus. Colliery is behind. Trolleybuses had been used between here and Conisbrough since 1916

G. Warnes

The turning circle at Manvers. M&S.T. Low bridge to the left under the MR with its road sign, also a good array of posters to cheer waiting passengers- ‘Give to fight polio”, ‘Belle Vue Zoo’, Sunfresh’, ‘Guinness’, ‘IPA’, one unreadable and ‘Players Please’.

C.T. Goode

The last tram to enter Barnsley & District Tramways service, No. 14, at Brush works, Louighborough before delivery.
Courtesy: Yorkshire Traction Co Ltd

It was No.26 which left Barnsley at 9.10 pm. with Driver Jim Bacon and Conductress Turton, arriving back at the depot at 1.40 am. on Sunday with a staff guard of honour waiting and thirteen passengers on board including a young lad with a coconut. Mr Nokes came by motor from home in Upton to Wombwell to drive the car to Thurnscoe and back, as he had done on the first day. Mr. R. Coutts, general manager and J. Seabrook, traffic superintendent, travelled part of the way. Belle of the hour, however, was Mrs. Coutts who completed the round trip alone, so as to obtain the last ticket issued. Mr Coutts, who rode from Thurnscoe, caused great merriment by stating that he was asked for his pass by the conductress, but admitted with shame that he had forgotten it!

Other publications by the author:

(* denotes those that are out fo print but which may be in stock or available in libraries.)

'The Mexborough & Swinton Traction Company'.*

'The Burton & Ashby Light Railway'.

'Railways in South Yorkshire'.*

'Railways of North Lincs'.

'The Wakefield, Pontefract & Goole Railway'.

'The Railways of Castleford'.

'Huddersfield Branch Lines'.

The Railways of Hull'.

'The Selby & Driffield Railway'.

'To the Crystal Palace'. (Forge Books)

'To the Alexandra Palace'. (Forge Books)

'Trentham, the Gardens and Branch Railway'.

'Doncaster's Trams & Trolleybuses'.